Compositions
for Flute

Matthew Leigh EMBLETON (b1978)

Copyright ©2020 Matthew Leigh Embleton. All rights reserved.

Compositions for Flute

Op 01 Journey in d-minor 4
Op 02 Nocturnes in d-minor and e-minor 5
Op 03 From Depth in a-minor 7
Op 04 Nocturnes in f-minor and g-minor 8
Op 05 Small Floating Crafts in c-minor 10
Op 06 Journey in a-minor 13
Op 07 Journey in c-minor 16
Op 08 Nocturne in c-minor 20
Op 10 Extransience in d-minor 22
Op 11 Victoria Park, December 2005 in e-minor (Version 2) 23
Op 12 Late Night Sky in g-minor 24
Op 13 Introduction in g-minor 26

Acknowledgments

Thanks to Attilia Mazzola for your collaboration, feedback, support, encouragement, friendship, and your fantastic recordings.

Thanks to the special people in my life who have supported and encouraged me in my work. Thank you for believing in me. You know who you are.

Matthew Leigh Embleton (b1978)   Compositions for Flute

Op 01 Journey in d-minor

01 Introduction, *piano con affetto*

02 The Pursuit, *con affetto e un poco agitato*

03 Looking Skyward, *con larghezza*

©2012, 2013, 2015, and 2020 Matthew Leigh Embleton

Op 02 Nocturnes in d-minor and e-minor

01 Nocturne in d-minor, *piano molto e cantabile*

Matthew Leigh Embleton (b1978) — Compositions for Flute

02 Nocturne in e-minor, *piano molto e cantabile*

Matthew Leigh Embleton (b1978)   Compositions for Flute

Op 03 From Depth in a-minor

Piano molto e penseroso

©2012, 2013, 2015, and 2020 Matthew Leigh Embleton

Matthew Leigh Embleton (b1978) Compositions for Flute

Op 04 Nocturnes in f-minor and g-minor

01 Nocturne in f-minor, *piano molto e cantabile*

02 Nocturne in g-minor (Version 1), *piano molto e cantabile*

©2012, 2013, 2015, and 2020 Matthew Leigh Embleton

Matthew Leigh Embleton (b1978) Compositions for Flute

02 Nocturne in g-minor (Version 2), *piano molto e cantabile*

©2012, 2013, 2015, and 2020 Matthew Leigh Embleton

Matthew Leigh Embleton (b1978) Compositions for Flute

Op 05 Small Floating Crafts in c-minor

01 Introduction, *con rubato e improvvisazione*

©2012, 2013, 2015, and 2020 Matthew Leigh Embleton

Matthew Leigh Embleton (b1978) — Compositions for Flute

02 Interlude, *con rubato e improvvisazione*

©2012, 2013, 2015, and 2020 Matthew Leigh Embleton

Matthew Leigh Embleton (b1978) — Compositions for Flute

03 Conclusion, *con rubato e improvvisazione*

Matthew Leigh Embleton (b1978)   Compositions for Flute

Op 06 Journey in a-minor

01 Arpeggiata, *adagio andante e piano*

02 Cloud Level (Version 2), *piano molto e penseroso*

©2012, 2013, 2015, and 2020 Matthew Leigh Embleton

Compositions for Flute

Matthew Leigh Embleton (b1978)

03 Eternal Recurrence, *piano molto con affetuoso*

©2012, 2013, 2015, and 2020 Matthew Leigh Embleton

Matthew Leigh Embleton (b1978) — Compositions for Flute

Op 07 Journey in c-minor

01 Introduction, *andante*

©2012, 2013, 2015, and 2020 Matthew Leigh Embleton

Matthew Leigh Embleton (b1978) Compositions for Flute

02 Interlude, *adagio*

©2012, 2013, 2015, and 2020 Matthew Leigh Embleton

Matthew Leigh Embleton (b1978) — Compositions for Flute

03 Conclusion, *allegro*

©2012, 2013, 2015, and 2020 Matthew Leigh Embleton

Matthew Leigh Embleton (b1978) Compositions for Flute

Op 08 Nocturne in c-minor

Piano molto e cantabile

©2012, 2013, 2015, and 2020 Matthew Leigh Embleton

Op 10 Extransience in d-minor

Affrettando con poco agitato

Op 11 Victoria Park, December 2005 in e-minor (Version 2)

Piano molto e penseroso

Matthew Leigh Embleton (b1978) Compositions for Flute

Op 12 Late Night Sky in g-minor

Piano molto e penseroso

©2012, 2013, 2015, and 2020 Matthew Leigh Embleton

Op 13 Introduction in g-minor

Piano molto e cantabile